James' Poems

Words

James Allen Spisak

First published by Dog Ear Publishing
4011 Vincennes Rd
Indianapolis, IN 46268
www.dogearpublishing.net

ISBN: 978-1-4575-3819-3

This book is printed on acid-free paper.

Printed in the United States of America

DEDICATION

This published book of
my poetry is dedicated to my
beautiful granddaughter
Danielle Nicole Spisak
1990-2013
in her loving memory.

01
"My Twin Brother"

On the day I was born
my dad planted a tiny Maple seedling.
Maybe it was coincidental, but as I grew up
I began to think of that tree as my twin brother,
certainly not an identical twin.
Dad nurtured us and fed us well,
even to the point of giving us vitamins.
Like most kids we went through childhood illnesses.
For me it was measles,
for my brother it was beetles,
both required the care of a doctor.
Dad was strict and disciplined with us both,
for me extra chores and for my brother, well,
he was tied to a stake,
Dad said he had to learn to grow straight.
Of course we celebrated our birthdays together.
At first I would run out and stand next to my brother
to see who was taller.
After a year or two I stopped of course.
My brother was very good-looking
and had a great build.
Each fall he would have his hair colored.
It was then we both had blond hair
his a bit more golden than mine.
I would worry about my brother,
especially during the winter
or even during a summer lightning storm,
but we both survived the test.

We were messy kids, especially in the fall.
There was no one else to gather the shedding of his locks
but me, but isn't that what brothers are for?
When my brother was old enough
and strong enough, Dad fastened
a swing to one of his arms. I am sure my brother was
happy to join in our fun.
As I became a man and fell in love,
I stood beneath my brother's arms, and with my wife to
be, carved a heart upon his side on
which we placed our hands, prayed,
and pledged our love.
Secretly I thanked my father
for the only brother I would have.
I know my dad is proud of me, and I of my twin brother
who is more than just a tree.
He's my brother.

02
"Talent"

We thank God for the gift of our senses,
for it takes all of them to appreciate the
fullness of His Creation.

Perhaps talent, this innate ability
to perform, is but one more of them.

Gifted not to all, but to a special few,
and not without cost, a lifetime of
practice in the quest for perfection.

Theirs becomes a life-long search
for the song that lies locked and
hidden in the keys of a piano,
the strings of a violin,
the chords of a human voice.

Only then when they have found the
purity and the perfection of their song
will they be satisfied.
And we will be grateful for their
shared talent.

03
"Words"

Webster owns and gives home to
more than thirty thousand of us.

We've come from different lands, and
our numbers continue to grow.

We are unique, yet have multiple
personalities that help hide who we are.
We are free, there is no charge for
our use, but our use comes with this
warning. We refuse to take back
whatever you say or write, it's the
nature of our existence.
We ask only that you not harm others
by what you say or write. Make us
proud, for we are all here to love
and serve one another.

04
"Time Out"

As a child, discipline for me was kneeling
in the corner of the family dining room.

Always the same corner, always facing the wall.

Flowers in the wallpaper
remain fixed in my memory,
every leaf, every petal, every flower
in my limited view.

For me, the time-outs allowed me to think
and reflect on my misdeeds.
I realized there are consequences for our actions,
and punishment was part of it.

No longer a child, no longer banished to the corner.
But there will always be value in time-outs
even if self-imposed.
No longer for the punishment of deeds
but a time out of life to just think,
to reflect, and maybe, yes, maybe to change.

05
"Nursing the Little Ones"

The smile she wore was genuine
and her voice, soft and gentle.
She spoke a soft pillow of words
for his tiny head to lay upon,
this little boy of four.
His hand remained within her grasp
long after he found sleep.

Satisfied, she left his side, this boy of four.
There is more to do, and night is long.
For in a room nearby lies a girl of five
who hasn't yet found sleep.
It's a soft pillow of words she needs
and a gentle hand to grasp,
this little girl of five.

06
"Reality"

Lies, somewhere between optimism
and pessimism, yet independent of both.

It's there to tell you,
you cannot afford that ring.

That puzzle piece won't fit,
no matter how you force it.

That gold necklace is just too
tangled to save – so give it up.

It's there to tell you if your relationship
will continue to work.

Please, won't someone help?
Find that place reality lies.

07
"Heartless"

The Heartless aren't born without a
heart, but one that is artificial.

Mechanically, it works, but only for
the functions for life.

Its bloodless flow renders them a
spiritless soul.

Destined to spend their lives on a
list awaiting a real one, which will
never come, except from that
unsuspecting soul, willing to give them theirs.

08
"Autumn"

Gradually it begins, the teasing of an unquenchable
desire for more. More of nature's artifact of
her trees and their spectacular blaze of color.

Impatiently we await the crescendo of color
that will explode upon the scene.

Not at night, but in the light of day, when
an Autumn sun will accent the beauty
of this gift from a loving God and
His farewell tribute to Summer.

09
"The Art of Being Subtle"

Like the softly-sung words
of a love song that lingers in one's thoughts,
is the subtle wisp of a woman's scent
lingering the air and nudging the senses,
long after she has passed by.

It was her purpose, for a woman knows the art and
craft of being subtle.
Clever and cunning are her ways and actions,
a skill sharpened by time.
Akin to the wiles of being seductive,
yet delicate and discrete.
It's saying without saying, but inferring her
not-so-obvious intent.
This the art of being subtle.

10
"Space"

Some call it Ether, even the brilliant of
minds, Einstein, was intrigued and
challenged by its existence.

Other than matter, it is the largest of
His creation. It is the absolute of nothing.

Is it eternal, as He is eternal,
or did it come about in creation that
matter would have a place to live?

Why, but why is there so much of it;
for God creates nothing without
purpose, unless there are more of us
somewhere out there in"Space."

11
"Circles"

There is a special beauty in things that
are round, for they exist without a flaw of line
or a beginning or end.

We can see it in our companions,
the moon and the sun.
It's always a circle in which our world travels,
that assures us we will not get lost.

The very existence of circles
began with a large bang.
And like a stone thrown into a placid lake that causes a ring
of circles, so, too, did our Creator,
by the event of His creation,
make fall, matter into the emptiness of space where an
endless ripple of circles
reaches out into a sea of emptiness.

It is within the center of this circle
that all life began.
This is the center of all that there is.
Could this be the home of our Creator and our God?
Could this be the place we call Heaven?

12
"Silence"

As darkness is the absence of light and white the
absence of color, silence is the absence of sound
and the opposite of noise.

Like space, silence is part of His creation
both sacred and pure.
It's balm for the grieving
and comfort for the troubled.

Silence is where writers of song and verse
find inspiration.
Choose silence as a friend,
it's there you'll find our Lord, speaking to you,
in the silence.

13
"Determination"

How sad this day has begun. There is no
morning art to greet me. Sun's paintbrush
of sunlight is either too bashful or held by
the lingering clouds of night.

But look, it's determined to free itself.
It has pushed aside its final restraint.

I am much stronger and determined than
any of you, says the sun.
This day the sun will shine,
whether you like it or not.

14
"The Heart of a Poet"

Blessed is the heart of a poet.
For it is from their heart,
beautiful words of poetry are written.
words, that speak of things others feel
and see, but can't find the words.
words, that tell of joy or sorrow like no other.
words, that laugh at you and make you laugh.
words, that change a rainy day
into a rainbow on a hill.
words, that can see a woman, there in a sunset.
words, that can describe the beauty
and scent of a woman.
But sad is the heart of a poet, who cannot find
words to tell of HIS love.
Oh, where now poet, is your way with words?

15
"Rituals of the Birds"

Aren't they fun, just to watch?
The males are again feeding their dates dinner.
And we all know what will come of that!

Interesting how we humans have adopted
the same ritual when we take our dates
and feed them dinner.

And we all know what can come of that!

16
"The Buds of Spring"

So swift is the change from one season to another,
and it happens in the blink of an eye.

So take the time, a moment will do,
and see and hear this change.
Today, I took that moment, in truth it took me.

The leaves are now gone, all gone but one,
and I wonder why this is so.
It's the leaves of the Oak that remain
Stubborn and unyielding, refusing the order to fall.
"You'll not intimidate me," says the Oak.
"I am the first of His trees,
and my fruit has fed mankind.
His favor rests upon me and my leaves,
and they are mine to keep
until the buds of Spring push them off."

17
"A Violin"
Dedicated to Kelly Braun
with Grandpa's love.

Nothing speaks the way a violin does.
It's the voice of an orchestra and of a song.

Tenderly, like no other, its voice carries,
the feeling, there in each note, each tender note.

It's the voice of an angel living there
in the strings of her violin.

18
"A Sacred Love"

Our hearts have been cloned with the love
that lives within the Sacred Heart of Jesus.

A love Incarnate with His Heavenly Father.

It's there, in the temple of each heart,
we find the love of the Holy Spirit.

19
"Trivial & Insignificant"

These are words that speak to things and times
we choose to label unimportant and of little value.

Be careful, please, be careful how you label
things and times.

Search again, sweet memory
of all that I have labeled so.

Regrettably, the memory was searched
and none were found.

Oh, how sad, never but never will there be another
chance to remember our trivial
and insignificant things and times.

20
"The Perfect Gift"

Love, is that perfect gift, and it comes
from the Heart of Our Lord.

Unconditional, unearned, given to those
of us in an imperfect world.

There in each breath we take.
So breathe deeply of His Love.
It's there in the perfect gift.

21
"Companions on a Journey"

Not always, are they the same, or is it, that we
notice, different, signs of change?

The breeze from the South had turned the corner
and decided its allegiance was to be from the
North. No longer gentle, but harsh, upon the face.

There, flown South, was a flock of birds,
on the wing of a North wind accompanied by a flock of
maple leaves.

The journey of the leaves, was short-lived,
but for the moment, they, too, were caught up in their
desire to fly South, with the friends they had lived,
when the sun was warm,
and high in the Summer sky.

22
"The Woman in the Sunset"

She will be there, she's always there in every
evening's sunset, on a bay, a bay in Naples.

Gracefully, she will arrive wearing an elegant
gown of unimaginable colors.

Her face, as radiant as the sun itself.

Occasionally she may wear a veil upon her face.

Her arms reach across the horizon, as if to
embrace all who have come.
Her bodice seems to embody the greatest
intensity of the color.

Her gown is sequined with diamonds, twisting
the light it reflects from the waters that pass by.
Her hem teases the sand,
curling like ruffles on a woman's dress.

Brief is her stay, before long she will close her eyes
and disappear over the horizon, to rest until tomorrow,
when the woman in the sunset will again display her
beauty for the people of Naples Bay.

23
"The Black Scarf, Part 1"

The elevator doors opened, but none departed.
There, stood another, who wanted on.

Could room be made for just one more?

Her face was that of an angel, framed by an
elegant black scarf.

Her green eyes met with mine,
and my smile her invitation.

Come, there is room enough for you.

With grace she entered, returned my smile,
and stood just inches from my touch.

It was her scarf that carried the fresh scent of a
woman, its purpose never in doubt.

She chose to dress for beauty, not for glamour,
the scarf indicated so.

Suddenly, the encounter was over, the doors were
again open, she was gone.

Her walk was swift, but before moving out of sight,
a breeze lifted the scarf, as if to wave a good-bye.
Perhaps we'll meet again.

"The Black Scarf, Part 2"

The elevator doors opened again,
my hope had been, she would be there.

The only thing there was my memory of her,
that face, framed by a black scarf.

Disappointed, yes, I am that.

Can one be disappointed in fate?
Of course they can.

No, it's my fault, I must begin a search for her.

There must be another way. Perhaps I should
begin to pray, yes, I'll pray.

"The Black Scarf, Part 3"

Yes, I prayed, prayed for guidance
guidance in finding her.

I now have a goal, it's the best friend a man can have,
for goals are the drivers of life.

It was here in this very building,
she entered my life and my space.

It was the elevator that brought her to me
perhaps by the elevator I shall find her!

"The Black Scarf, Part 4: The Wait"

From where did she come?

I am not a Sherlock Holmes,
but by sheer deduction of
certain facts, I can begin my search.

It was late Friday afternoon about 5:00 PM.
I had been to see my publisher on the 10th floor.

She boarded the elevator on the 5th.

Floors one through five are used for doctor offices.

Could she be, a patient, a receptionist, a nurse,
or perhaps a doctor?

To find out, I will time a wait,
Friday, 5:00 PM, the 5th floor.

With anticipation and some anxiety I will wait!!!

"The Black Scarf, Part 5: The Meeting"

I timed my wait for Friday, the fifth floor,
precisely at five.

I trust my Sherlockian deduction of facts will lead her to
me. Will fate finally make it so?

So, there I stood, waiting,
when suddenly it happened,
as I prayed it would.
It was the Black Scarf she wore that caught my eye. Her
path, would lead her directly to me.
What would I say?
Just how do you speak to an angel?

Awestruck, I let my smile speak for me... And so it was,
with neither a word from either of us,
our smiles spoke for us.

We boarded the elevator and stood side by side.

We turned to each other, our smiles ensued.
I reached for her hand, and she was willing.
It's you, yes, it's me.
Our hearts were united as one
a union made possible
by a mere smile and a Black Scarf.

24
"The Dance of the Leaves"

Could there be a more beautiful
day than today? I don't think so!

There is enough inspiration to
last one a lifetime.

Sometimes we ask,
haven't we seen it all?
But the more we watch, the more
we see, and the more we see,
the more we appreciate the
gifts of His Love.

Today, I watched many a leaf
dance their way to their end.

Some seemed to hold the hand of another
as they danced their way.
Never were they trained for this, but instinctively
they knew the dance, some waltzed,
others spun their way.
Those from the tallest danced the longest.
We were called early, one said, others will
follow, you can count on it.
It's been that way from the beginning.

25
"The Flower Garden"

When I awake, He plants a thought and gives
me time to think. I struggle for words to write,
eventually He pities me and tells me what to
write. Today He planted a seed into my
garden of thoughts. I've left it grow and now
have these words to share.

Life is more than a garden of roses. It is a
vast, endless garden of every imaginable flower –
every color, every size, a delight within itself.

The Gardener, yes, the Gardener, how He loves His
garden and His flowers. He knows them all,
and they know Him.

When they are thirsty, He gives them drink.
From time to time He will pick some to take
home with Him, almost unknown to the others.
Quickly, their place is filled by the younger plants.
His garden is old, but seems never to change.

Unlike all the other gardens, the flowers
picked from this garden will never die as long
as they are with Him.

26
"Opportunities"

We hope, pray, practice, and train for one,
then we wait and wait for that certain set
of circumstances we call an opportunity.

Yet, opportunities are not all self-serving.
There is another, for which we don't pray,
don't practice, train, or wait.

It's the opportunity of the heart calling us to
serve as the Good Samaritan served.
For His was an opportunity of the heart
and love for someone in need.

So, in our wait, let not a cry for help
become just another missed opportunity.

27
"The Daffodil"
dedicated to my Betty Lou

Dear Flower of Spring, we have waited
so long for your arrival.

Now, we feel there is hope
hope for each new beginning.

We see it there, in the smile on your face.

Don't hurry away, stay with us, stay as
long as you can; for our wait is long
until we see you again.

Fret not your lack of fragrance.
It's your beauty that has won our favor.

28
"The Snowflake"

Given birth, a gift from a chosen cloud.

Offspring without color, yet full of beauty,
like a field of diamonds
pure and flawless.

Designs by the Master.

Like man, no two ever the same.

This, the "Magnificent Snowflake."

29
"A Woman"

A woman is more than synonymous with love
and beauty, a woman *is* love and beauty.

A gift from God, made not from dust or dirt,
but from the rib of man.

Thus, she became the crème de la crème
of His creation.

Not any poem, nor verse or song can
ever describe, the beauty of
this gift, this gift of a woman.

30
"My Friend"

There is a special pen I have.
It's not too fat or too slim.
It doesn't write too dark or too light, but just right.

I remember the day I found it,
and we've been friends ever since.

Its ink flows, like the blood that flows
in the fingers of my hand.

When I am sad, my friend picks me up and writes such
hopeful things.

I just hope it doesn't run out of ink
before it runs out of words.

31
"Put on a Happy Face"

Pain is a simple word, but not easy to describe.
For us, it becomes a row of tiny faces, used to show
the face we feel is ours.

As I left my doctor's office,
I began to look into the face of
each stranger. Some I saw as a one or two.
There is a five,
oh my, I can see a ten over there!

Ironically, the number ten seemed to be a wealthy woman,
but she wore the face of a ten.

The number one and two were quite the opposite. Both had
little means, at least by their attire.

The question, how do number ten faces
become a number one or two?

Quite simply, they "Put on a Happy Face."

32
"Peace"

It's calm and serene,
like a placid lake on a moonlit night.

It's a soft and gentle rain
from a non-threatening sky.
It's snowflakes that take twice as long to fall from
a windless sky.

It's quiet, it's free of noise.

There is no hostility here, for we are
in agreement with our God, and we are at peace.

33
"Farewell for Now"

The artist paints upon a canvas in
colors of red, green, and gold.

On pages of a journal, a poet writes
words in shades of humor, love, and sadness.

The Saints often died for their faith.
You have died unto yourself for your values.

You have chosen sackcloth for now,
but one day, yes, one day, you shall wear silk.

34
"Poetic Bliss"

The words of poetry
often become the lyrics of a Song.

All others remain to live a life of celibacy,
where only the reading of words remain.

But the words of a poet, that find a mate, are
destined to live on, united, in "Songs of Love."

35
"Bit"

The word itself is tiny, in fact it's just a bit.
It's what our world is made of, yes,
we are a mosaic of tiny bits.

Each bit of us is different and speaks to
our uniqueness. It tells who we are
and reveals if it was I that was there.
A bit, a small part launched many careers.
Bit by bit they struggled to find success.
Not found in one large piece, but in the
sum total of their life's tiny bits.

36
"The Beauty of the Night"

Come early, and watch night prepare itself
for an evening of enchantment.

Watch day grudgingly give back its
last, and night like a blotter
happy to get it back.

The set is alive with creatures tuning
their instruments for tonight's concert.

Special effects have now signaled the moon to
cast its light upon the set.

Trees are basking in the lime light of the moon,
twisting and turning like ladies in a chorus line.

Do they move at the whim of a breeze, or have
they saved some energy from the light of day?

Look, lightning bugs are now on the scene.
Their flash bulbs capturing
"the beauty of the night."

Now, aren't you glad you decided to come early
and stay late?

37
"Farewell to Another Season"

Leaves are almost gone, the frost has
already been upon the pumpkin,
and the fodder is there in the shock.

The view, is much more open now,
and the veil of leaves, nearly gone.

Preparations have been made for Winter,
and the set has been designed.

It will again be pure white, no color, just white.

38
"If Only It Could Speak"

I looked upon this simple dollar bill,
quite worn from all its use.
If only it could speak, I thought
there must be many stories it could tell.

I closed my eyes and pictured a
a little boy, clutching it in
his precious little hand.

A gift of love from his grandfather,
to be saved or spent.
By now it's crumpled into a ball
as he hands it to the clerk.
He choose to spend it on a treat
But where next will it go, this simple dollar bill?
Will it ever know love like that again, as the day
it was placed into the hand of a little boy?

39
"Words to Live By"

"I love you."
Three words that are from the Divine,
the source of all love.
"I love you, and will lay down my life
for you."

"Thank you."
But where are the other nine?
We must not live the lives of the nine,
but as the one who said "Thank you."

"I am sorry."
It must be said and from the heart. This
and this alone will earn forgiveness.
Why is it so hard to say these words?
We must learn to say them, and say
them often. It is these words that
will get us to where we long to go.

40
"Imagination"

Oh, this gift of imagination, this plantation,
this field of thoughts and dreams.

Euphoric fantasies,
without bounds
without class
without charge.

Now, we must pray, pray it can be so.
Then, yes, then, imagine it will be so.

41
"Our Voices"

Unique as the simple, but magnificent snowflake
or man himself is the voice
God has placed within us.

Unique for His purpose, for God creates nothing
without purpose.

Unique says we're different,
yet we remain the same.

Our voice is one of those unique features,
for when we pray to our Lord, He knows
who prayed. He knows us by "Our Voice."

42
"Morning Art"

An exhibit, a fresco, seen upon the side
of a house or a garage door.

Painted by the brush of sunlight upon a tree.

A bird lands upon its branch, and there it is,
captured in its shadow.

43
"Poetic License"

Is it liberty or immunity that allows a poet or
artist to deviate from the norm and still,
remain acceptable?
No, it's their poetic license to do so.
It's a freedom of behavior that allows
their brush or pen to speak that which is
in their heart.

The diplomat has his immunity,
the artist and poet their poetic license.
So let the impressionist's brush paint upon a canvas,
let the poet, his pen upon a page.

And where does this poetic license come?
But the eye of the beholder, who sees beauty
in each of their works.

44
"Not Just Another Day"

They're given to us in increments of time,
one day, one day at a time.

And who is it we are to thank
for the gift of this day,
but the One who has given us the rest of
all else, the rest of everything?

The giver of days gives them freely, and
never are they meant to waste.
Tomorrow cannot be lived today, and yesterday
cannot be lived again.
Today is the only day we can be certain of
It's another day to serve others
as He has served us.
Another day to love, not hate.
Another day to write, to paint, and to sing.
Another day to plant and harvest.
Another day to make love and conceive new life.
Another day to hear the cry of new life.
Another day to visit the sick and bury the dead.
D-Day may have started as just another day,
but it's not the way it ended.
Sept. 11th may have started as just another day,
but it's not the way it ended.
Never, never think of each new day as just another day,
God help those who do!
There is so much for us to do, and we may have only today
in which to do it!

45
"Refresh in Me"

Refresh in me these gifts that stir,
for they are there to sanctify, complete, and make perfect
each virtue that lies within.

It is by these virtues we will do God's work through us and
by the power of the Holy Spirit.

So, refresh in me Your gift of Wisdom
that I may know of the truth
and be able to see the whole image of God.

Refresh in me Your gift of Understanding,
that I will not be confused
by anything other than the truth,
for self-evident principles
are known by "common sense" found within
Your gift of understanding.

Refresh in me Your gift of Counsel, that I may always know
right from wrong
and choose to do what is right.

Refresh in me Your gift of Fortitude, for with this gift I will
find the courage to
follow Jesus, in spite of all rejection.

Refresh in me Your gift of Knowledge,
that I may grow to know all that has
been revealed by the "Word" Jesus.

Refresh in me Your gift of Piety,
for by this gift I may show my love by my
reverence and sense of respect
for my God and the Church.

Refresh in me Your gift of Fear of the Lord,
for it is by the sheer awe of God
that we are aware of His glory and majesty.
He is the perfection of all we desire.

So, refresh in me
refresh in me these gifts that set me free.

46
"Trees"

Inspired must be the words we choose to
write of this gift.

Reverently we must speak of their greatness
and beauty.

They boldly stand from the tallest reds to smallest.

They feed the hungry and provide our shelter.

They help decorate what man has chosen to build.

It is with trees He chose to landscape the jewel of His
creation, our planet Earth.

Like hands in prayer, they reach for the heavens.

They worship for all of us in their unending prayer of
thanksgiving to their Creator and our God.

47
"The Seasons"

We are all born to live and participate in nature's
four-act play, "The Seasons."

The longest running of any play, choreographed
and presented on a stage as big as life itself.

Supported by a cast of billions.

Each act brings to us sets of unimaginable
proportions.

A musical score unprecedented
An audience mesmerized by its sheer beauty.

And its theme of love, by its director,
forms the background of purpose, that we may love one
another and the creation of a loving God.

48
"Life at Betty's Feeder"

There seems to be a sadness within her
birds today, and I wonder why!

Fewer are coming for breakfast, and those
that do, seem unhappy.
There is no excitement,
they eat now for survival.

Because I sense their sadness,
I, too, have become saddened.

I ponder this, and conclude, they
are sad because so many of their
friends have flown south.

Only the faithful and hardened
of the flocks remain.

There was a Cardinal and a Blue Jay
side by side eating breakfast.
I wish I could read beaks as some do lips.
The Cardinal seems to be saying to the Blue Jay,
I tried to talk them into staying
I said there is always seed at Betty's feeder
and you are always welcome. It isn't that,
it isn't that at all. We would love to stay,
but there is an urge within, and we must fly to
where that urge takes us.

49
"The Season for Weddings"

The season of weddings is a time for giving gifts.
Please, take time before you choose
a gift of money.
Instead, create for the couple, a memory,
and the memory you create will become your gift.

A wedding gift should always be well-chosen
and always accompanied with beautiful
words that match the beauty of your gift.

Be assured, both will become for them
a memory of your love and thoughtfulness.
This the purpose of your gift.

50
"The Moodiness of Rain"

I can always tell the mood you're in each
time I hear you rain.

When you're angry, you're torrential.

When you could care less, you are but a drizzle.

And when you are melancholy and caring,
you are gentle, very gentle.

51
"The Sound of a Clock"

For some the sound of a clock brings comfort as
it pronounces the passage of time.

So I followed the sound, in search of the clock
that I might know of its time.

Finally, I found it, but not its time,
for upon its face there were no hands
Lost was its purpose, except for the
comfort it continues to bring
as it pronounces the passage of time.

52
"Friday Afternoons"

Fifty-two of them each year, and thank God
for every one of them.
They can never come soon enough,
to make life tolerable.
A time to rest, a true time-out.
The rubber band of stress, relaxed moments
before it was about to break.
I know it's bad, but not that bad.
I know I can make it.
Thank God I still have a job!

53
"Dust"

Insignificant perhaps,
but dust is really no small matter.
Never welcomed, always uninvited,
we lack the power to deprive it of its right
to accumulate, especially on things we value so.
We know it's there, we can see it there,
and our finger confirms how much is there.
Its invasion into our homes and lives
will never end.
Sadly, the lives of many valued
possessions are lost, at the hand of
a careless duster.
I can think of no other nuisance,
hated and despised as much as dust,
except for its first cousin, lint.

54
"It Happens Each Spring"

Something happens each Spring, and it
happens because of a flower, a Daffodil.

You've introduced the world to Spring,
and now there is Hope.
Your purpose has been fulfilled.
Now it's time for the others in His garden
to awaken.

Your time to flower has ended,
your last flower has fallen.
Our wait again will be long, but we trust
something will happen in the Spring,
and it happens every Spring, because of you.

55
"Worth It"

If we could have but ten years
of togetherness, would it be worth it?
Of course it would.

If we could have but five years
of togetherness, would it be worth it?
Of course it would.

If we could have but one year
of togetherness, would it be worth it?
Of course it would.

If we could have but one day
of togetherness, would it be worth it?
Of course it would.

We can only live one day of
the future at a time,
yet even one day, just one day
of togetherness would be worth it.

56
"Fall's Annual Fashion Show"

The annual fall fashion show is about to begin.
Worn by the stars of this gala event are the maples,
the oak, the beech, the hickory, and the aspen.
Fashions worn are designed by the renounced designer
known to all as "Padre"
For fall He has chosen gorgeous reds,
yellows and golds,
and a magical hue of the three.
Fashions are to be worn for this single event
and none to be saved.
Models will disrobe in humble modesty
as their garments fall to the ground.
They have earned a rest from their summer work,
but will awake in the Spring.
A bit shy at first, their buds will peek out before they will
fully dress, in a garment of green for
the annual event know as Summer

57
"A Love Story"

The story of this man is not mine,
but believe it to be true.
My story is mine and mine to tell.

There was a man, not a young man, but advanced. He was
prayerful, but never did anyone see him pray from a book
or from anything.
One day a man was moved and curious by what he saw.
What was it he prayed and always
without a book? Eventually he had to ask,
what is it you pray?
The man looked up, from a face at peace.
I pray but one word.
I pray the name of Jesus.
Over and over I pray that one word.

As a poet, I was amazed with his accomplishment.
I, too, avoid unnecessary words in my works.
It is the fewest of words that
results in the purist of verses, just read the Proverbs.
Could I, as he, find the fewest of words as a writer?
Which one, which word would it be?
Yes, of course, I know the word.
It's the word love! Over and over I have written of it.
No sooner I spoke the
words I thought of His word! Oh, my God!
Say them James,
say them together, say love Jesus.
There it was, the heart and soul
of every verse and song, and the reason for both.
Go ahead say the words and keep saying them.

58
"A Cornucopia of Gifts"

We say variety is the spice of life! It's far
more than that; it's the substance of life itself.
It's more than one bird to see or one song to hear.
More than one face to love or one food to eat.
It's more of anything, you could ever imagine.
So look about, and see there is more than one.
More than one of everything.
Thank you, Lord, yes, thank you
for this cornucopia, Your cornucopia of gifts.

59
"Choreographed to Dance"

Tomorrow has come, and I am ready to write.

There is barely a breeze, in fact it's almost calm.

There is movement in the leaves,
but oh, so slight, not even close to a rustle,
but simply the dancing of the leaves.

Not from any power of their own, but
choreographed to dance at the whim of a breeze.

60
"A Poem"

A poem begins as a thought, a seedling
planted in the womb of the mind.

There, thoughtful meditation continues
to feed its growth and journey into life.

And when gestation is complete, there
is a birth. A thought is given a life of its
own as a poem, the offspring of a poet.

Now, clothed in its unique garment of
words, it lives on to share with you its story.

61
"Experience Defines the Word"

It's funny, how certain words are so clearly
understood that a dictionary isn't needed
to define what they mean.

Love is such a word, in fact what does a
dictionary know of its meaning if it never
experienced it?

Love never has been a word one can
define, for it needs to be
experienced to understand its true meaning.

It can be found, in kindness, it's there,
you will find love in abundance, and your
experience will define the word
Love..

62
"Prayers"

The most thoughtful gift we can give
a friend is to pray for them.

There are those who seek the prayers
of the Saints, for they are in the presence of God.

But the prayers of a friend are greater than these.

For it is by their Faith and Trust they pray.

63
"Sunrise & Sunset"

The sun neither rises nor sets.
It's we who turn our faces from the light of its sun.

It's we who tire of the light and must rest.

Rested, we again turn our face to the
light of a new day.

Never alone, we need only reach for His hand.

In His care, He will guide us in living our new day.

64
"Hands"

Oh, these hands that we have been so blessed,
for they are the heart of our very existence.
They are an extension of our heart's love.
A perfect set of utensils,
crafted by the Master, Himself.

They bless us, they are the hand of the surgeon, they are
the hand that holds the hand of a dying parent.
They are a mother's hands for the life-long caring of God's
gift, her children. They are a father's hands, who provides
substance for the lives of his family.
The hands of a man in love,
caressing the breast of his loved one.
They are the hands of the artist and musician
giving praise to God with their works. They are the hands
that speak to the deaf. They are the hands of the caregiver
doing God's work.
They are the hands of our military holding weapons in
defense of our Country.
They are the hands that reach out in friendship.

They are the hands of our Priest
elevating the Eucharist and Chalice,
the precious Body and Blood of our Lord Jesus,
the perfect Sacrifice of our Liturgy, the Mass.

Father, thank you for the gift of our "Hands"

65
"Prelude"

The genesis of "Harmony" is the beautiful
word itself. You simply find peace in just
saying the word.
I hope my words have found the peace that
lies within it.

66
"Harmony"

It's peace and love we find in the harmony
of the Father, Son, and Holy Spirit.
A harmony of three in one.

One creation by one God.
In harmony throughout the universe,
a constant within all of His creation.

May He have said, "Let there be harmony
in all I have created for you and in you."

Peace awaits all those who live
in harmony with me.

67
"A Blank Sheet of Paper"

From the time I was given the life of a sheet of paper,
I've patiently waited and wondered
by whom and how will I be called to serve.

Of the billions of blank sheets, what are the chances of
being chosen to serve the author of a
Gettysburg Address or to have recorded on one's self the
notes of an Albert Einstein's
theory of relativity or perhaps be
privy to the tender feelings of someone in love?

The ways and the times are countless,
and opportunity awaits, yet fear remains present, the fear
of being called upon to record the wasted ramblings of a
God-forsaken doodler.

That, however, will never be my destiny,
for but a moment ago, a bond was formed with a man
called James, who began this very verse,
the verse of a poet.

He has my gratitude, for no longer will I be
just a blank sheet of paper.

67
"Weeds"

I've always thought the worst nuisance in life
was that of dust, lint, and perhaps those horrible potholes.

But I've come to realize that it's none of these;
it's the existence of weeds.

Their invasion into our gardens
and our lives is relentless.
It's an undeclared war, that's what it is.

Our arsenal of weapons
has become greater than ever.
This unrelenting force for their extinction continues.

But in fairness, let's step back and rethink this.
Aren't we the invaders of their space?

All they are trying to do
is reclaim their right to exist.
We have all the weapons,
and theirs is just a desire to survive.

Now they live in constant fear of the hand of the
dreaded gardener intent on ending their lives.

68
"Gifts"

Never in doubt, should there be
in the existence of our God,
this God of love we call Father.
It's by His gifts, that we know of Him.
Like Him, His gifts have neither a beginning
nor an end.
It's there in the gift of healing, the promise
of hope, in each sunrise followed
by a daily shower of gifts.
It's there in the cry of a newborn,
a gift, a new life.
It's there in the gift of reason, that we know
and believe in Him.
It's there in the gift of talents, that we sing,
that we paint, that we write of the
"Word" made flesh.
It's there in the perfect gift of Christmas,
the Christ Child.
Custodians we remain of all His gifts, never
meant to waste, only to share.

Never will we out-give the Giver of gifts.
Remember always, the gift and sacrifice
of His Son, that we may have eternal life,
there in the care of His love.

69
"Procrastination"

The ultimate inhibitor of progress and change.
A malady, an illness that results in the status quo
and a task for tomorrow.

For a group, a people, or a country, only
leadership can overcome its trappings of
mind and will.

For the individual, a promise,
a commitment; for whenever there is
something important to be done,
we must do it, that's all there is to it.

70
"A New Year"

Truly a gift, this new year, never used,
crisp as a new dollar bill,
anxious to be spent.

Forget the past year, it's gone,
but remember the good you
learned of life, it is this we must build upon.

One more year, to get it right
God knows how many more there will be.

Wealth is OK, if it be the result of arduous toil
and shared with the less fortunate.

Remember, focus on the eye of the needle, through
which we must pass and be judged.

71
"Things"

Things, yes, things, innocuous, yet oh,
so prominent a part of our lives.

Compulsively we buy them, collect,
save, and even fight over them.

"You heard me, keep your hands off
my things."

Things are everything that has a claim
to their own existence, for they exist
without life.

In the end, we remain grateful, to have
something that remains, to remind us
of a better day and a fond memory.

Lord, we thank you, for it's from Your
bounty we have all our "Things."

72
"The Morning Dove"

I am there each morning
long before all the others.
There to practice my song, but not yet
good enough to join the choir that sings all day.
Never will I give up. I dream that my day
will have a happy ending.
Perhaps tomorrow, yes, tomorrow is another day.
I want more, than the morning to sing.

But if He wants me to do no more than
this, I will be grateful and proud to be
His morning dove.

73
"My Porch"

My porch is my refuge,
screened-in but not screened
out from the sights and sounds that bring peace,
real peace.

Without notice, the scenes change
as seasons, come and go.

It's my place to think, and to write.
A place to look inward, and to pray.

We all should have a porch such as mine,
but it's mine, and you'll have to find one for yourself.

74
"Change"

Dying suggests change – is that why we
fear it so?

Change is never easy, even when
that change is good for us.

We are comfortable in our sameness,
in spite of its crosses.

We would rather wear sackcloth than
silk, and all because we hate
and fear the uncertainty of change.

75
"You Are There"

You, yes, you are there.
In my thoughts, you are there.

You arrive each day on the crest of a breeze.
You are there in the song of His birds,
the scent of flowers.

You are there in the porcelain blue of His sky.

You are there in everything that is good.
And everything that is good is there in you.

It's you that is there, the woman you are
is the woman that is there.

76
"My Favorite Rest Stop"

It's my porch of course, where the air is free.
You can use as much as you want or need,
and it's open 24/7, holidays included.
The Attendant happens to be imaginary,
but that's OK,
cause He sure is a good listener and lets you talk as
long as you want.
You must learn to give Him time to speak, however Just,
be quiet and listen, for His voice is soft and gentle.
I've learned to trust in what He tells me,
and I always
feel much better and rested when I leave.
I just love that Attendant of mine.

77
"Adopt a Need"

Thoughts of adoption come when the
heart is touched to share the love within it.
To share and give our love to
a child of another.
This may not be possible in many cases,
but adoption has other forms that are
noble and pleasing to God.
The needs of many are great, yet the
needs of a friend must never be ignored.
So let our hearts be touched by their
needs. Let us be moved to adopt their
need in our prayers, for the greatest gift
we can give a friend is to pray for them
and their needs. The only obligation that
remains is a prayer of thanksgiving
when that prayer has been answered.

78
"Called First"

How ironic it is, that we seem to spend
our lives, trying to be first, when
Our Lord tells us, it is the first who
will be called last and the last
called first.

Shouldn't we, at least find out what it
means to be last, so we can be called first?

79
"Just in Time"

Some say he was a man ahead of
his (Time).

I guess he just didn't want to waste
(Time).

His mom would remind him, "Take
your (Time), you have a life (Time)
to finish that."

In truth he was a generous man and
never said no to those who asked for
some of his (Time).

Sadly, I heard he died. I guess his
(Time) had just run out.

I did learn, that before he passed away,
he finally took some (Time) off. He did
go on a vacation, where it is said, he had
(The Time of His Life).

80
"Sacrifice"

It's because we love, that we sacrifice,
and because we sacrifice that we love.

Meanings the same, for love
cannot exist, without sacrifice.

It was there, in the forfeiture of a Son,
for the sake of a someone, a someone like me.

81
"Valley of Tears"

A simple wound seems to heal itself
and often does.
If only it was that easy; for we know
there is no greater need than healing.
Much greater than prayers for wealth
are those for healing.
This Valley of Tears, in which we live
is lined with those who cry out.
The One they cry out to is no
stranger to our Valley.
Our Lord walked its paths and healed
many along His way.
In the end, He was its victim.
Totally innocent of any wrongdoing,
yet ravaged by His own people.
This for us and our salvation, He
suffered, died, and was buried. He rose
from the dead and from His
Valley of Tears.
Trust in Him, for He hears our cries.
His love for us is there in the palm
of His Healing Hand.
We need but reach for it.

82
"The Ethic for Work"

Is said to be a set of values,
based on hard work and diligence.

From where does it come, this ethic,
and when does it begin?

Like a butterfly, emerging from its cocoon,
is the life of a child
who has reached the age of accountability,
the age of reason.

The butterfly leaves its cocoon, full of color,
gloriously flying into life with a purpose.

After seven years of development,
a child emerges into life
as a unique person, with a personality of their own.

This is the time, we must plant a purpose
into their young minds.

By a simple and gradual assignment of tasks, life will begin
to have purpose, then a set of values, based on work,
will become their ethic for work.

83
"Cloud Nine"

Cloud Nine is where I want to go, not just me,
but you and me.
Where the clouds are cottony soft as the
softness of your face.
So on a plane we'll go, it's no further than
nine I am told.
Close to Heaven they say,
and like in Heaven we'll be.
It's where we must go. I'll buy our tickets
when you say yes.
So honey, it's a trip you'll never forget.
Close those blue eyes of yours
and imagine this place, this place called
Cloud Nine.

Snippets

01
"Her Silhouette"

As a circle is the purist of lines, it
is the magic in the lines of a Silhouette
that will capture the beauty of a face,
her face, her Silhouette.

02
"Gentleness"

Speak softly of the word itself.

There is no weakness here, only strength

and kindness to be found.

A gift, gently planted by the Hand of its Maker.

03
"Creation"

A "Big Bang" announced His creation.

The gifts of all life buried there, in a single atom.

The gestation of all life,
a mere fourteen billion years.

Thus we call Him God and Father.

04
"Praying twice"

You write, and your heart is given a voice.

You sing, and you pray twice.

05
"The Greedy Investors"

The hungry buyers returned to the market
like birds to a feeder, only to be spooked
by who knows what or why.

06
"Season of Grief"

It's cold, and shadows, long. Days were stolen
of their light, darkness controls everything.

When, when will the Hope of Spring
replace this dreaded
"Season of Grief?"

07
"Eternity"

When time gives way to Eternity, it gives
back all our yesterdays, and sacrifices all
our tomorrows, that we may remain
forever in the here and now.

08
"For Whom"

Did God create trees for the Birds or
Birds for the trees?

I believe He made both of them for Us.

09
"Service"

We live in the Service of others.
This alone is our greatest prayer.

For it is the highest level of our
existence and most pleasing to our God.

10
"Food for Thought"

Are things the way they are because it is
what it is or because we allow it to be so?

Our will is free and we can change things
to be what they should be,
and not what they are.
Even the time purchased from a simple
parking meter is too valuable to waste.
We can discover the secret of why it's
better to give than receive when we try it.

11

Life is a tug-of-war, somewhere between
I am sorry, and thank you.

It's there, you'll find yourself, in the
middle, of all of it.

————————

Words hoarded, have little value, until they
are spent and shared.

————————————————————

In poetry, the fewer the words
the better the verse.
And so it is in life, when these few words,
I love you, mean so much.

————————————————————

12

The most frequent thing we do in life
is make choices.

Life comes to us, not as a complete
package, but à la carte.

A separate price for each choice.

————————————————————————————————

You know that you are on the right track
and headed in the right direction when
the good fortune of your neighbor
turns from envy to gladness.

————————————————————————————————

Where on earth can certainty be found
if not in the here and now?

Look up, it's there, for certain it's there.
It's always been there and will always be there.

————————————————————————————————

13

Dawn plays its Prelude song with
birds announcing the start of a new day.

————————————————————————————————

We find comfort in our sameness,
but boredom in the lifestyle we let it create.

————————————————————————————————

Do more than stop and smell the roses.
Pick some and share their heavenly
fragrance with someone you love.

————————————————————————————————

14

Out of love, not duty, changes everything.

Have you ever wondered, who may have
been the first to utter the words
I love you?
I believe only God knows who that may have been.

Our heads are made to look ahead.
There is no future in looking back

15
"A Precious Moment"

No real value, brighter than gold
this bouquet of dandelions, and the words,
"Here mommy, I picked these for you."

16
"The Chickadee"

By size it's one of the smallest,
but its song one of the finest.

A song that befits its name,
the song of the Chickadee.

17
"Imagination"

Is but a blackboard, where the images
of the mind appear.

Swiftly, you erase one, and there is
another, another, and another.

18
"The Inkwell"

Only the ink that flows from the
inkwell of the heart can write
words of love.

Words, not of this ink, will render
lines of empty words, empty of love.

19
"A Dome"

I spent some time this afternoon on
my porch. There to give my mind a breath
of fresh air. All I could think of, was the
beautiful Spring day we had been
so blessed. There under a dome,
a dome of porcelain blue.

20
"A Season for Everything"

Blessed are we with a season and
a time for everything.

Purposely, He created our planet Earth,
so things would not always stay the same,
but gracefully move from one season to
another, giving us a season and
a time for everything.

21
"Imagination"

It must be imagined before it can be so.

Blessed are the thinkers
for discovery lies within their thoughts
and in their imagination.

22
"A Streak of Imagination"

Is like a falling star, that dies and keeps on dying.

Only to leave behind the imagination of
a poet in words that will live and keep on living.

23
"An Email Marriage"

Is one in which age matters not,

where looks and appearances
are never a problem, where words matter.

Come to think of it, it's words
that matter in every marriage.

24
"A Thought for the Day"

It's one thing to think nice things.
It's even better when you say them.

25
"Time"

Where, but where will time
take us, or can it take us anywhere?

No, no, time cannot take us, for it has no mind or
will of its own but can be led anywhere its master
wishes to go.

26
"When"

When you're thirsty can you tell
yourself you're not?
When you're cold can you tell
yourself you're not?
When you're hungry can you tell
yourself you're not?
And when you're tired can you tell
yourself you're not?
No,
nor can you tell yourself life
is over when it's not.

27
"A Day Doing Nothing"

Because we are alive, we must live each day.
There are no days or weekends off from life.
It's our minds that refuse to do no thing.
They remain busy, thinking of
all our yesterdays and hopes for all our tomorrows.
So much, for a day of doing nothing.

28
"Our Feelings"

There are so many of them,
and I wonder about each.
Yet these are the things that
will lead us around.
Like a dog on a walk, they pull
and yank us to where they want us to go.
Are they in control of us or
we in control of them?
Only time will tell whose
will is the strongest.

29
"So Let Them Speak"

In addition to their fragrance
and beauty, flowers have
a voice of their own,
so let them speak for you.

30
"A Thought"

The chasm between lust
and love is ever so deep,
yet the distance between
is ever so slight.

CPSIA information can be obtained
at www.ICGtesting.com
Printed in the USA
LVHW111842140119
603857LV00002B/498/P